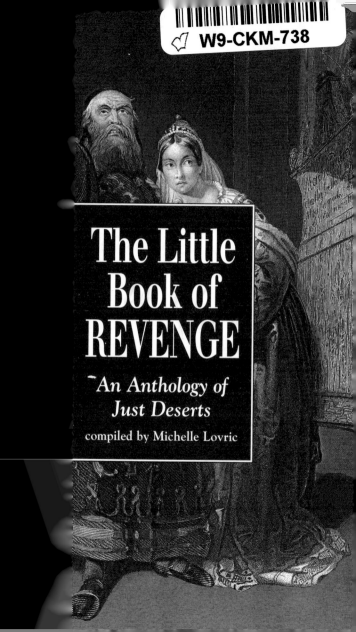

The Little Book of REVENGE

An Anthology of Just Deserts

compiled by Michelle Lovric

introduction

No one doubts the piquant flavour of a sweet revenge, or the satisfaction it gives when we see a malefactor receive his just deserts.

Anyone who commits a hurtful act must spend some time looking over his shoulder. The wheel of fortune seems most often to deliver a penalty to wrong-doers. As the Samoan proverb goes, "Today my turn, tomorrow yours."

Not surprisingly, revenge has been the subject of many important myths and legends, and formed the backbone of the plots of plays, operas and novels.

Writers have dipped their pens in poison to exact retribution for slights, real and imagined. Wags have played practical jokes. Spurned lovers and betrayed spouses look to avenge themselves with means commensurate with and appropriate to the style of their betrayal. One of the most pungent forms of revenge is the curse. Every culture has developed its own repertoire of dread imprecations, the mere utterance of which is often a full revenge.

CONTENTS
contents

sweet revenge

To be revenged on an enemy
is to obtain a second life.

Publius Syrus (fl. 43 BC)
Roman epigrammatist and compiler

Enemies to me are the sauce piquant
to my dish of life.

Elsa Maxwell (1883–1963)
American hostess, writer and broadcaster

It [revenge] is sweeter far than flowing honey.

Homer (fl. 1000 BC)
Greek epic poet

Vengeance is mine; I will repay, saith the Lord.
Therefore if thine enemy hunger, feed him;
if he thirst, give him drink: for in so doing
thou shalt heap coals of fire on his head.

The Holy Bible, New Testament: Romans, xii, 19, 20

Revenge is profitable, gratitude is expensive.

Edward Gibbon (1737–94)
English historian

Che ga in boca l'amaro no pol spuar dolce.
He who has a bitter taste in his mouth
cannot belch sweetly.

Venetian proverb

softly softly

Revenge is a luscious fruit
which you must leave to ripen.

Emile Gaboriau (1835–73)
French novelist

Meekness, *n.* Uncommon patience in
planning a revenge that is worth while.

Ambrose Bierce (1842–1914)
American journalist and writer

Though your enemy is the size of an ant,
regard him as an elephant.

Danish proverb

 If you can't bite,
better not show your teeth.

Yiddish proverb

Now Vengeance has a brood of eggs,
But Patience must be hen.

George Meredith (1828–1909)
English novelist and poet

Though the mills of God grind slowly,
yet they grind exceeding small;
Though with patience he stands waiting,
with exactness grinds he all.

Friedrich von Logau (1604–55)
German poet and epigrammatist

softly softly

Vengeance comes not slowly either upon you
or any other wicked man, but steals silently
and imperceptibly, placing its foot on the bad.

Euripides (c. 480–406 BC)
Greek dramatist

"Vengeance is good, sweeter than life itself."
Yes, so say the ignorant.

Decimus Junius Juvenal (AD 40–125)
Roman satirical poet

One generally hates people
that one is in the wrong with.

From a letter by Lady Sarah Lennox, great-granddaughter of Charles II of England,
to Lady Susan O'Brien, July 7th, 1761.

A man that studieth revenge keeps
his own wounds green, which otherwise
would heal and do well.

Francis Bacon (1561–1626)
English statesman, essayist and philosopher

History too clearly proves that the
holiest of causes have often been lost
when the fury of vengeance has
taken possession of men.

From a letter by George Sand (Amantine Aurore Dudevant) (1804–76),
French woman of letters, in a protest inserted in the Paris newspaper
La Liberté, after threats of prosecution to journalists for publishing
part of her novel *Cadio*, September 23rd, 1867.

In the physical world anything which
strikes is subjected to the same force in
reaction; but in the moral world the
reaction is stronger than the action.
The reaction from being imposed upon is
scorn; the reaction from scorn is hatred;
the reaction from hatred is murder …

Giacomo Girolamo Casanova (1725–98)
Italian adventurer

an eye for an eye

Eye for eye, tooth for tooth,
hand for hand, foot for foot.

The Holy Bible, Old Testament: Deuteronomy, xix, 21

It will have blood; they say,
blood will have blood.

William Shakespeare (1564–1616)
English poet and playwright, from *Macbeth*

They have sown the wind, and they
shall reap the whirlwind.

The Holy Bible, Old Testament: Hosea, viii, 7

Whatever any one desires from another,
the same returns upon himself.

Ralph Waldo Emerson (1803–82)
American writer

He that diggeth a pit shall fall into it.

The Holy Bible, Old Testament: Ecclesiastes, x, 8

He that sows iniquity shall reap sorrow.

Thomas Fuller (1608–61)
English clergyman

Once in an age the biter
should be bit.

Thomas d'Urfey (1653–1723)
English poet and dramatist

You arrive Mr. Big Shot
but leave Mr. Nobody.

Zulu proverb

Among the Anglo-Saxons a subject conceiving himself wronged by the king was permitted, on proving his injury, to beat a brazen image of the royal offender with a switch that was afterward applied to his own naked back. The latter rite was performed by the public hangman, and it assured moderation in the plaintiff's choice of switch.

Ambrose Bierce (1842–1914)
American journalist and writer

In Greek legend, the Furies are three goddesses of vengeance who castigate all transgressors. Considered by some to be the daughters of Gaea and Uranus and by others to be daughters of the Night, they continue to punish their victims even after death. Their names are Tisiphone (the Avenger of Blood), Alecto (the Implacable) and Megaera (the Jealous One).

Acis is crushed to death with a rock and then changed into a river by Polyphemus the Cyclops, his rival for the love of Galatea.

In Greek mythology, the huntsman
Actaeon is changed into a stag and
torn to pieces by the goddess Diana's
hounds after he sees her bathing.

In Greek legend, Arachne hangs herself
after losing a weaving contest to the
goddess Athene. Athene then changes
Arachne into a spider – hence Arachnida,
the scientific name for spiders.

Phaedra falls in love with her stepson
Hippolytus, but when her love is unrequited,
she slanders him to her husband Theseus,
who has him killed. Full of remorse,
Phaedra later kills herself.

Odysseus returns from his travels
to find his wife surrounded by
insolent importuning suitors.
He therefore disguises himself
so that he can despatch them all.

When Agamemnon, leader of
the Greeks at the siege of Troy,
returns from the battle with
Cassandra, the daughter of King
Priam, he is killed by his wife
Clytemnestra and her lover
Aegisthus. Agamemnon's daughter,
Electra, persuades her brother
Orestes to avenge their father's
death by killing Clytemnestra and
her paramour.

Pluto has told Proserpina that she can only return to the upper world if she refuses all food. However, Ascalaphus sees her eating a pomegranate and tells Pluto. In revenge, Proserpina turns Ascalaphus into an owl.

Oedipus is the son of Laius and Jocasta, the King and Queen of Thebes. It is prophesized that Oedipus will murder his father and marry his mother. To avoid this outcome he is abandoned as a baby and brought up by shepherds. However, when he has grown up, he unwittingly kills Laius, and, when he solves the riddle of the Sphinx, becomes King of Thebes and thereby entitled to marry Jocasta. Horrified at the fulfilment of the prophesy, Jocasta hangs herself and Oedipus puts his own eyes out.

Salome agrees to perform the Dance of the Seven Veils for Herod so that he will grant her one wish: to bring her the head of John the Baptist, who has spurned her.

In the story of Samson and Delilah, the hero is a warrior of Israel attempting to shake off the yoke of the Philistines. Abimelech, Satrap of Gaza, insults the downtrodden people and Samson avenges them by killing him. Delilah, hating him for a previous rejection, seduces him and betrays him, cutting off his hair and thereby destroying his strength.

The legend of the curse of Tutankhamun arises from the death of the fifth Earl of Carnarvon during the excavations of the tomb. Although he died from a mosquito bite, spiritualists, including Sir Arthur Conan Doyle, have suggested that his death could have been caused by a curse uttered by the priests of the dead Pharaoh. Strange coincidences, such as the simultaneous death of Carnarvon's dog in England and a power cut in Cairo, have contributed to this legend.

The Pied Piper of Hamlyn offers to help the town rid itself of a plague of rats for a fee of 100 Marks. However, once he has carried out the task, the townspeople refuse to pay him. In revenge he plays his pipe to lure all the children into a cave in a hillside which closes around them. The parents never see their children again.

Hansel and Gretel are captured by a wicked witch who eats children. They manage to escape and push the witch into her own oven where she is cooked as a gingerbread cake.

some scenes from grand opera

In Georges Bizet's *Carmen* Don José stabs the seductive gypsy girl Carmen who has betrayed his love.

In *Fedora* by Umberto Giordana, based on Victorien Sardou's play *The Russian Princess*, Fedora Romazoff swears to avenge the murder of her lover. She tracks the suspect Loris to Paris, spies on him for the authorities and seduces him, only to have him confess to the killing, but explain that it was done honourably, for her betrothed was an evil scoundrel. Fedora falls in love with Loris, but the trap she had formerly laid for him is now closing around them. They escape, but Loris's mother and brother become victims of the revenge that she had once planned for him. Forced to confess she is the spy who betrayed him, she swallows poison from the Byzantine cross she always wears, and dies.

In *Habanera* by Raoul Laparra, two brothers harbour a desperate passion for the same woman. Pilar loves Pedro and Ramón kills him. With his dying gasp, Pedro places a curse on his brother, to be carried out on the anniversary of the murder. On the due date Pedro's ghost appears and sends his brother mad, while Pilar expires and joins her lover in heaven.

In *Lucrezia Borgia* by Gaetano Donizetti (based on Victor Hugo's drama) the Duchess of Ferrara accidentally poisons her own illegitimate son during a wholesale poisoning of her noble enemies at a banquet.

In Mozart's *Don Giovanni* (libretto by Lorenzo Da Ponte) the wicked libertine Don kills the father of a girl he is trying to seduce forcibly. He later insults the statue of his victim, which comes to life and warns of retribution. The Don laughs off the warning, but at a banquet the next day the statue appears. Don Giovanni refuses to repent and the statue suddenly vanishes, the ground opens up and a horde of demons appear and bear the libertine down to the fiery gulph of hell.

some scenes from grand opera

In *Il Trovatore* or *The Gypsy's Vengeance* by Giuseppe Verdi, a gypsy woman is burnt at the stake for allegedly bewitching the infant brother of the Count di Luna. Her daughter Azucena steals the baby and intends to throw it into the same fire. Deranged by grief she accidentally consigns her own child to the flames and is left to bring up the infant nobleman Manrico as her own. When he grows up, Manrico falls in love with the Countess Leonora. His rival for her hand proves to be his own brother, the Count di Luna. The two brothers duel; 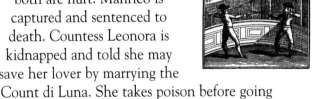 both are hurt. Manrico is captured and sentenced to death. Countess Leonora is kidnapped and told she may save her lover by marrying the Count di Luna. She takes poison before going to set her lover free. She dies in the arms of Manrico, who, not caring to live without Leonora, is led to his execution. At last Azucena is able to reveal his identity – and her revenge – to the grief-stricken Count.

some literary feuds

At a public dinner, in the days when England and France were mortal enemies, the poet, Thomas Campbell proposed the health of Napoleon Bonaparte, Emperor of the French. The company was astounded, and when the poet was asked how he could make such a toast, he replied: "Because he once shot a bookseller!"

"No, I am not dead, and I would like to imprint proof of my unequivocal existence on your shoulders with a very vigorous stick. I would do so, in fact, did I not fear the plague miasma of your mephitic corpse."

From a letter by the Marquis de Sade (1740–1814), French writer, to a columnist for the journal *Ami des Lois*, 1799, following the publication of a premature obituary in which the journalist had slated de Sade's scandalous novel *Justine*.

When American satirist Dorothy Parker met Clare Booth Luce, a fellow writer, in a doorway, Booth Luce made way saying: "Age before Beauty." Parker swept ahead, retorting: "Pearls before Swine."

"The Comtesse de Brémont presents her compliments to Mr W. S. Gilbert and in reply to his answer to her request for an interview for St. Paul's in which he states his terms as twenty guineas for that privilege, begs to say that she anticipates the pleasure of writing his obituary for nothing."

From a letter by the Comtesse de Brémont to the nineteenth-century librettist William Schwenck Gilbert after he had informed her that if she wanted to interview him, she would have to pay a fee of twenty guineas.

I have received your new book against the human race. I thank you for it. You will please mankind to whom you tell a few home truths but you will not correct it. You depict with very true colours the horrors of human society which out of ignorance and weakness sets its hopes on so many comforts. Never has so much wit been used in an attempt to make us like animals. The desire to walk on all fours seizes one when one reads your work.

From a letter by Voltaire (François-Marie Arouet) (1694–1778), French writer, to Jean-Jacques Rousseau, 1755, after Voltaire had received a copy of Rousseau's *Discourse on the Origin of Inequality among Men*, which advanced the notion of the superiority of primitive life to that of civilization.

I am only one, only one, only one. Only one being, one at the same time. Not two, not three, only one. Only one life to live, only sixty minutes in one hour. Only one pair of eyes. Only one brain. Only one being. Being only one, having only one pair of eyes, having only one time, having only one life, I cannot read your MS. three or four times. Not even one time. Only one look, only one look is enough. Hardly one copy would sell here. Hardly one. Hardly one. Many thanks. I am returning the MS. by registered post. Only one MS. by one post.

From a rejection letter by a London publisher to the American writer Gertrude Stein (1874–1946). The publisher was clearly not impressed by her repetitive prose style ("a rose is rose is a rose …").

John Keats
(1795–1821)
This Grave
contains all that was Mortal
of a
YOUNG ENGLISH POET
Who
on his Death Bed,
in the Bitterness of his Heart
at the Malicious Power of his enemies,
desired
these Words to be engraved on his Tomb Stone.
"Here lies One
Whose name was writ in Water."

Rome, Italy

29

You have undertaken to cheat me. I will not sue you because the law takes too long. I will ruin you.

From a letter by the nineteenth-century American railroad tycoon Cornelius Vanderbilt to a man who had acted dishonourably with him.

May your hens take the disorder (the fowl-pest), your cows the crippen (phosphorosis), and your calves the white scour! May yourself go stone-blind so that you will not know your wife from a haystack!

A famous curse given by a rate collector, Willis, to an Irish farmer, Murphy, who refused to pay his dues, date unknown.

Pox, piles and a heavy vengeance!

English curse, sixteenth and seventeenth century

Never come near me again!
you are a faithless cur, and may the
hangman take all faithless curs.

From a letter by Ludwig van Beethoven (1770–1827), German composer,
to his old friend, Nepomuk Hummel, 1799.

My dearest Nazerl,
You are an honest fellow and I now perceive
you were right; so come to see me this
afternoon; Schhuppanzigh will be here too,
and the pair of us will scold you, cuff you
and shake you to your heart's content.
A warm embrace from your Beethoven
also known as Little Dumpling

Beethoven to Hummel the following day.

You are a pretty fellow, truly, not to have written
to me for these two months. Have you forgotten
who I am, and the rank I hold in the family?
I shall make you remember this, young man; and,
if you irritate me, I shall reduce you to the ranks.
You knew I was on the point of lying-in; and you
care no more about my health than if I were still
a girl. Well, I have to inform you, and you may
storm at the intelligence as much as you please,
that I am brought to bed of a son, who shall suck
hatred to you with his milk, and that I intend to
have a great many more, for the sole purpose
of raising you up enemies.

From a letter dated March 15th, 1649, by Madame Marie de Sévigné
(1626–96), French woman of letters, to her cousin, Count de Bussy Rabutin,
who became a maliciously disappointed suitor in her widowhood.

I would like to daub your
beard with glue and
decorate it with all the
bits of fluff I have removed
from my old Hoover.

From an anonymous letter to the television critic
Elkan Allan, published in *The Sunday Times*.

Remember,
if you write anything nasty about me,
I'll come round and blow up your toilet.

Courtney Love
Contemporary American singer

Oh, you little wretch! your
letter cost me fourpence. I will
pull all the plums out of your
puddings; I will undress your
dolls and steal their under
petticoats; you shall have no
currant-jelly to your rice; I will
kiss you till you cannot see out of
your eyes; when nobody else
whips you, I will do so; I will
fill you so full of sugar-plums
that they shall run out of your
nose and ears; lastly, your frocks shall
be so short that they shall not come below
your knees. Your loving grandfather,

SYDNEY SMITH

The Reverend Sydney Smith (1771–1845), English clergyman,
essayist and wit, threatens his little granddaughter with awful penalties
for omitting to stamp his letter properly.

Revenge is now the cud that I do chew.

Francis Beaumont (1584–1616) and John Fletcher (1579–1625)
English dramatists
from *Queen of Corinth*

Had all his hairs been lives,
my great revenge
Had stomach for them all.

William Shakespeare (1564–1616)
English poet and playwright
Othello on Iago in *Othello*

Vengeance is in my heart, death in my hand,
Blood and revenge are hammering in my head.

Aaron to Tamora in *Titus Andronicus*

By this leek, I will most horribly revenge.

Pistol to Fluellen in *Henry V*

marital strife

If you want to get revenge on a man,
marry him!

Basia Briggs

I don't suppose any married man exists
who hasn't at one time wished his wife dead!

Lord Millais as quoted by the English artist Vanessa Bell in a letter to Margery
Snowden, March 15th, 1903. According to Vanessa Bell, Lady Millais was present
when he made this comment.

Men who consistently leave the toilet seat up
secretly want women to get up to go to the
bathroom in the middle of the night and fall in.

Rita Rudner (b. 1955)
American comedienne

Burning dinner is not
incompetence but war.

Marge Piercy (b. 1936)
American writer

Morning screams to you.
[a marriage curse]

Irish curse

My fame has enabled me to torture
more formidable men.

Sharon Stone (b. 1958)
American actress

I think she merits equal praise
That has the wit to bite the biter.

Edward Ward (1667–1731)
English humorist
from *Nuptial Dialogues*

MARITAL STRIFE

marital strife

Forgiveness and a smile is the best revenge.

Samuel Palmer (1741–1813)
English essayist and biographer

Frustrated groom Cyril Snipe threw a can of
paint over his 79-year-old girlfriend's house,
causing £4000 worth of damage, after she
cancelled their wedding for a third time.
Cyril, also aged 79, said: "We split up and she
rings me up again. I still love the woman, but
now I think it's best if it ends."

THE FOLLOWING ADVERTISEMENT APPEARED IN
THE CONNECTICUT COURANT IN 1806:

Thomas Hutchins has advertised, that I have absented myself from his bed and board, and forbid all persons trusting me on his account, and cautioned all persons against making me any payment on his account. I now advertise the public that the same Thomas Hutchins came as a fortune-teller into this town about a year ago with a recommendation, which, with some artful falsehood, induced me to marry him. Of the four wives he had before me, the last he quarrelled away; how the other three came to their deaths, he can best inform the public; but I caution all widows or maidens against marrying him, be their desire for matrimony ever so strong. Should he make his advances under a feigned name, they may look out for a little, strutting, talkative, feeble, meagre, hatchet-faced fellow, with spindle shanks, and a little warped in the back.

In 1659 a great cull of unpleasant husbands took place in Rome. Investigations revealed that the young widows had received the help of an old Sicilian woman called Spara, the diligent pupil of an infamous poison-monger called Toffania who distributed her wares in small glass bottles decorated with the image of a saint. "Acqua Toffania" is thought to have consisted of crystallized arsenic dissolved in water. The brood of murderous wives was uncovered, arrested and tortured. Old Spara and five of her protegées were hanged.

They say you shouldn't say nothing about the dead unless it's good. He's dead. Good.

Jackie "Moms" Mabley (1894–1975)
American singer and comedienne

But there is another Reason why Women cuckold their Husbands, and that is out of Revenge. Now, revenge is Sweeter than Muscadine and Eggs; and can you blame Women for loving Sweet Things?

Edward Ward Gent
from *The Whole Pleasures of Matrimony*, 1743

the ex-factor

'Tis sweet to love;
but when with scorn we meet,
Revenge supplies the loss
with joys as great.

George Granville (1667–1735)
English poet and dramatist

After your fling
Watch for the sting.

Unknown

It is normal to want to ram his car
if he and his new girlfriend have
been spotted in it.

Helen Lederer
Contemporary English comedienne and writer

Never give back the ring.
Never. Swallow it first.

Joan Rivers (b. 1933)
American comedienne

the ex-factor

I like your Plan immensely of Extirpating that vile race of beings call'd man but I (who you know am clever (VERREE) clever) have thought of an improvement in the sistim suppose we were to Cut of [sic] their prominent members and by that means render them Harmless innofencive Little Creatures; We might have such charming vocal Music Every house might be Qualified to get up an opera and Piccinis Music would be still more in vogue than it is & we might make such usefull Animals of them in other Respects Consider Well this scheme.

From a letter by Maria Allen (c. 1750–?), to English writer Fanny Burney.

Don't waste time trying to break a man's heart; be satisfied if you can just manage to chip it in a brand new place.

Helen Rowland (1875–1950)
American journalist

One must be a woman to know how to revenge.

Madame de Rieux

Of course, a girl hates to wound a man; but sometimes, after a painful parting, it would seem so much more artistic if he would only remain "wounded" just a little longer.

Helen Rowland (1875–1950)
American journalist

the ex-factor

THIS NOTICE APPEARED IN AN IRISH NEWSPAPER
IN THE NINETEENTH CENTURY:

Run away from Patrick M'Dallagh.
– Whereas my wife, Mrs Bridgett M'Dallagh,
is again walked away with herself, and left
me with her four small children, and her
poor old blind mother, and nobody else to
look after house and home, and, I hear, has
taken up with Tom Gingan, the lame fiddler
– the same was put in the stocks last Easter
for stealing Barday Doody's game cock.
This is to give notice, that I will not pay for
bite or sup on her or his account to man or
mortal, and that she had better never show
the mark of her ten toes near my home again.

Patrick M'Dallagh

N.B. – Tom had better keep out of my sight.

AN EPITAPH

Here lies by wife POLLY, a terrible shrew;
If I said I was sorry, I should lie too.

Australia

practical jokes

In one of his notebooks, Leonardo da Vinci recalled the revenge of a fellow artist.

The artist was in his studio and had to endure the visit of an interfering priest, who insisted on sprinkling his paintings with holy water, much to their detriment. The painter was angry.

The priest claimed that he was not only doing his duty but furthermore a good deed, and whoever did a good deed should not expect abuse but a recompense as great or even greater from on high.

The priest eventually left the studio, and as he walked along the street, he was startled to be drenched with water, poured from a large bucket by the artist from his studio window. The artist crowed: "Here is your reward that comes to you a hundredfold from on high for your generous act of ruining my paintings."

The art historian Giorgio Vasari records that da Vinci also took revenge on a prior who constantly nagged and pressured him to work harder on his painting, *The Last Supper*, for the Dominican fathers in Milan. Da Vinci painted the prior's likeness for the face of Judas, and the resemblance was obvious to his patrons.

Giacomo Casanova, the legendary Venetian lover and adventurer, was angered by a practical joke which resulted in him falling into a mire. His revenge was sharp: that night he cut the arm off a freshly buried corpse and placed it in the bed of his foe. The unfortunate man suffered a stroke on seeing it, and never spoke again.

During the reign of George II, a most unusual wager was entered into by Lord Nugent, who swore to his friend Lord Temple that he would spit into the hat of the somewhat effeminate Earl of Bristol. He contrived to do so, as if by accident, and was treated civilly by Bristol as the incident took place at a fashionable gathering of the highest society. Lord Nugent considered that he had got away with his prank, until the next morning, when he received a challenge to a duel with Lord Bristol. Nothing would suffice to prevent bloodshed but that both Lords Nugent and Temple publicly begged pardon of Lord Bristol at White's Club.

Nathaniel Wraxall
from *Historical Memoirs*, 1836

I had the faults common to my age, was talkative, a glutton, and sometimes a liar ... I recollect, indeed, that one day, while Madam Clot, a neighbour of ours, was gone to church, I made water in her kettle; the remembrance even now makes me smile, for Madam Clot ... was one of the most tedious, grumbling old women I ever knew.

Jean Jacques Rousseau (1712–78)
French writer and philosopher

There was a boy in my class at school who always stood at the top, nor could I with all my efforts supplant him ... till at length I observed that when a question was asked him he always fumbled with his finger at a particular button on the lower part of his waistcoat. To remove it, therefore, became expedient in my eyes; and in an evil moment it was removed with a knife ... When the boy was again questioned, his fingers sought at once for the button, but it was not to be found. In his distress he looked down for it; it was to be seen no more than to be felt. He stood confounded, and I took possession of his place; nor did he ever recover it, or ever, I believe, suspect who was the author of his wrong. Often in after life has the sight of him smote me, as I passed by him ...

Sir Walter Scott (1771–1832)
Scottish novelist and poet

All these and similar escapades, however, were fairly eclipsed by the famous Berners Street hoax, which created such a sensation in London in 1809. By despatching several thousands of letters to innumerable quarters, [Theodore Hook] completely blocked up the entrance to the street, by an assemblage of the most heterogeneous kind. The parties written to had been requested to call on a certain day at the house of a lady, residing at No. 54 Berners Street, against whom Hook and one or two of his friends had conceived a grudge. So successful was the trick, that nearly all obeyed the summons. Coal-wagons, heavily-laden, carts of upholstery, cars with pianos and other articles, wedding and funeral coaches, all rumbled through, and filled up the adjoining streets and lanes; sweeps assembled with all the implements of their trade,

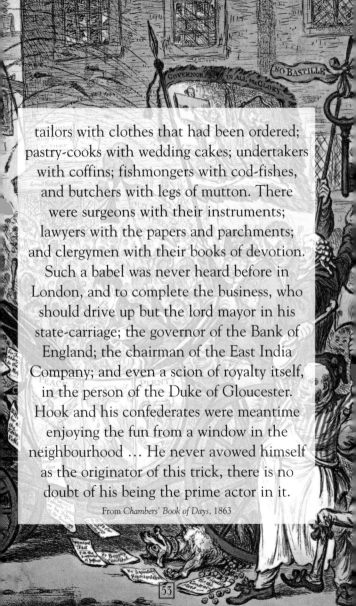

tailors with clothes that had been ordered; pastry-cooks with wedding cakes; undertakers with coffins; fishmongers with cod-fishes, and butchers with legs of mutton. There were surgeons with their instruments; lawyers with the papers and parchments; and clergymen with their books of devotion. Such a babel was never heard before in London, and to complete the business, who should drive up but the lord mayor in his state-carriage; the governor of the Bank of England; the chairman of the East India Company; and even a scion of royalty itself, in the person of the Duke of Gloucester. Hook and his confederates were meantime enjoying the fun from a window in the neighbourhood … He never avowed himself as the originator of this trick, there is no doubt of his being the prime actor in it.

From *Chambers' Book of Days*, 1863

Hit your head on a corner of a tofu and die!

Japanese curse

May you live in interesting times!

Chinese curse

It is my heart-warming and world-embracing Christmas hope and aspiration that all of us – the high, the low, the rich, the poor, the admired, the despised, the loved, the hated, the civilized, the savage – may eventually be gathered in a heaven of everlasting rest and peace and bliss – except the inventor of the telephone.

Mark Twain (Samuel Langhorne Clemens) (1835–1910)
American writer

May their bodies be cursed.
May they be cursed in the head and the brain.
May they be cursed in their eyes and their foreheads.
May they be cursed in their ears and their noses.
May they be cursed in fields and in pastures.
May they be cursed in the mouth and the throat,
cursed in the chest and the heart,
cursed in the stomach, cursed in the blood,
cursed in the hands and feet and in each of
their members.
May they be cursed going in and going out.
May they be cursed in towns and in castles.
May they be cursed in streets and in squares.
May they be cursed when sleeping and when awake,
when going out and returning,
when eating and drinking,
when speaking and being silent.
May they be cursed in all places and at all times.

Excommunication curse found at the Abbey of Fécamp, founded by
Duke Richard I of Normandy in 990.

Curses are like chickens; they come home to roost.

Greek proverb

"May the father who created man, curse him. – May the
Son who suffered for us, curse him. – May the Holy Ghost
who was given to us in baptism, curse him (Obadiah.) –
May the holy cross which Christ for our salvation
triumphing over his enemies, ascended, – curse him.

"May the holy and eternal Virgin Mary, mother of God,
curse him. – May St. Michael the advocate of holy souls,
curse him. – May all the angels and archangels, principalities
and powers, and all the heavenly armies, curse him." [Our
armies swore terribly in Flanders, cried my uncle Toby, –
but nothing to this. – For my own part, I could not have a
heart to curse my dog so.] ...

"May he (Obadiah) be damn'd where-ever he be, –
whether in the house or the stables, the garden or the
field, or the highway, or in the path, or in the wood, or in
the water, or in the church. – May he be cursed in living,
in dying." [Here my uncle Toby taking the advantage of a
minim in the second barr of his tune, kept whistling one
continual note to the end of the sentence – Dr. Slop with
his division of curses moving under him, like a running
bass all the way.] "May he be cursed in eating and drinking,
in being hungry, in being thirsty, in fasting, in sleeping,
in slumbering, in walking, in standing, in sitting, in lying,
in working, in resting, in pissing, in shitting,
and in blood-letting.

"May he (Obadiah) be cursed in all the faculties
of his body.

"May he be cursed inwardly and outwardly. – May
he be cursed in the hair of his head. – May he be
cursed in his brains, and in his vertex," (that is a
sad curse, quoth my father) "in his temples, in his
forehead, in his ears, in his eye-brows, in his cheeks,
in his jaw-bones, in his nostrils, in his foreteeth and
grinders, in his lips, in his throat, in his shoulders, in
his wrists, in his arms, in his hands, in his fingers.

"May he be damn'd in his mouth, in his breast, in his
heart, and purtenance, down to the very stomach.

"May he be cursed in his reins, and in his groin,"
(God in heaven forbid, quoth my uncle Toby) –
"in his thighs, in his genitals," (my father shook his
head) "and in his hips, and in his knees, his legs,
and feet, and toe-nails.

"May he be cursed in all the joints and articulations
of his members, from the top of his head to the soal
of his foot, may there be no soundness in him."

Laurence Sterne (1713–68)
Irish writer

May all the goats in Gorey
chase you to hell.

A curse on your house if you have one;
if you haven't, blast the stars.

May you be mangled!

Six horse-loads of graveyard clay
on top of you!

May the man who would curse the bladder
out of a goat have a chat with you before
Christmas.

Death and bad luck afterwards to you.

May you be torn in strips
and have a rag for a bonnet.

having the last word

Too many there be to whom
a dead enemy smells well,
and who find musk and amber in revenge.

Sir Thomas Browne (1605–82)
English physician and philosophical writer

You villains! if this stone you see,
Remember that you murdered me!
You bruised my head, and pierced my heart,
Also my bowels did suffer part.

Epitaph in St Michael's churchyard, Workington, Cumbria, 1808

I know what should be put on my tomb:
Died of the Neglect of his Correspondence
and Consequent Conscientitis.

Robert Louis Stevenson (1850–94)
Scottish writer

François Ravaillac (1578–1610), the assassin of the French King Henry IV, was found guilty of divine and human high treason. He was sentenced to have his skin torn with hot pincers and the wounds filled with molten lead and boiling oil. His right hand, holding the regicidal knife, was to be burned in a sulphur fire. Then he was to be torn to pieces, while still alive, by four horses, and to have his limbs reduced to ashes which would then be scattered to the winds. Ravaillac's request for a conditional absolution was granted, on the condition of eternal damnation if he turned out to have acted with accomplices, instead of alone, as he claimed. Ravaillac replied: "I receive absolution upon this condition."

Frederic Rowland Marvin
from *The Last Words of Distinguished Men and Women*, 1900

Robin Pemberton
Here lies ROBIN but not ROBIN HOOD;
Here lies ROBIN that never did good;
Here lies ROBIN by heav'n forsaken;
Here lies ROBIN – the Devil may take un.

Epitaph in South Shields, Tyne and Wear

And when you die, have
everything buried with you.
If the next wife wants it,
make her dig. I'm going
to have a mausoleum.
More closet space.

Joan Rivers (b. 1933)
American comedienne

God was very good to the world.
He took her from us.

Bette Davis (1908–89) on fellow American actress Miriam Hopkins.

last words

Well, I only hope he saved some of my money to pay for his funeral.

Maria Callas (1923–77), American operatic soprano,
on the death of her agent.

The reason why so many people showed up at Louis B. Meyer's funeral was they wanted to make sure he was dead.

Samuel Goldwyn (1882–1974)
Polish-born American film producer

May the only tears at your graveside be the onion-pullers'.

Irish curse

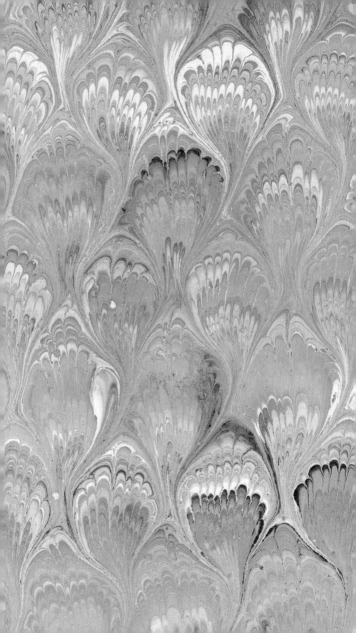